BOOK OF MORMON STORIES APPLIED TO CHILDREN

WHO'S YOUR HERO?

VOLUME 4

written and illustrated by
DAVID BOWMAN

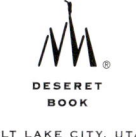

DESERET BOOK

SALT LAKE CITY, UTAH

"For I did liken all scriptures unto us,

that it might be for our profit and learning."

Nephi

Author's Note to Parents:

Who's Your Hero? is both an enjoyable children's book and a teaching tool. The "How can YOU be like . . ." pages and Family Home Evening Lesson Helps are designed to help you teach your children how the principles found within each story apply to them. I encourage you to take full advantage of these tools and watch how the heroes from the Book of Mormon come to life for your young ones. God bless.

David Bowman

CONTENTS

Lehi's Family (Most of Them)
  Holds Fast to the Word of God 1
  How can YOU be like Lehi and his family? 13
  Family Home Evening Lesson Helps 22

Amulek and Alma Cooperate 25
  How can YOU be like Amulek and Alma? 37
  Family Home Evening Lesson Helps 46

Mormon and Moroni
  Act Responsibly 49
  How can YOU be like Mormon and Moroni? ... 61
  Family Home Evening Lesson Helps 70

Other FHE Helps 72

LEHI'S FAMILY
(Most of Them)
Holds Fast to the Word of God

Greetings, friend! It's me, Lehi. One night, while my family and I were traveling through the wilderness, I had a special dream. It showed me how important it is to always HOLD FAST to the WORD of GOD.

In my dream I saw a huge field with many, many people. They were all trying to get to a tree that had white fruit. However, the fruit was not easy to get to! There were many ways for the people to get lost or distracted. (1 Nephi 8:2, 9–10)

I saw that the only ones who made it to the tree HELD FAST to a ROD of IRON the entire way.
(1 Nephi 8:30)

I walked up to the tree, pulled off a piece of fruit, and took a bite. It was delicious! It made me feel very good inside. More than anything, I wanted to share this fruit with my family. I looked around for them and saw my wife and sons far away. I waved for them to come and join me. (1 Nephi 8:11–15)

My wife, Sariah, and my two sons, Nephi and Sam, saw me waving and said, "Yes, we're coming!" But Laman and Lemuel, my two oldest sons, did not want to come. (Sigh!) Even in my dream they were acting like knuckleheads. (1 Nephi 8:16–18)

Nephi, Sariah, and Sam began their journey to the tree. The first thing they did was GRAB HOLD of the IRON ROD. It led them along a narrow path that would take them to the tree. With each step, they held on as tight as they could to the iron rod. (1 Nephi 8:14–16, 19–22)

Suddenly a thick mist of darkness surrounded my family! They couldn't see where they were going! So they gripped the iron rod even *tighter*, trusting that it would lead them to the tree. Other people who would not HOLD to the ROD wandered off and were lost in the darkness. (1 Nephi 8:23)

Next I saw a huge building filled with people in expensive clothes. They were laughing and trying to get those on the path to join them. To some, it looked like those people were having much more fun! They let go of the iron rod and started going toward the building. But instead they fell into a river of filthy water and drowned. (1 Nephi 8:26–27, 31–32)

My family followed the iron rod until they could finally see the tree. They had made it! Hooray! They saw people happily picking and eating the fruit. (1 Nephi 8:24)

Unfortunately, some of those people looked over toward the huge building. They saw the people in the building laughing and making fun of them for eating the fruit. Embarrassed, they tossed their fruit aside, walked away from the tree, and were lost. Can you believe it? (1 Nephi 8:25–28)

Nephi, Sam, Sariah, and I were not embarrassed. We enjoyed eating the fruit together and paid no attention to the people in the building. I was so happy to have my family there with me, even though I was very sad that Laman and Lemuel would not come. And I was grateful for the iron rod—without HOLDING FAST to the IRON ROD, we never could have made it to the tree. (1 Nephi 8:16, 35)

And then I woke up. I knew that this dream was from Heavenly Father and that it had special meaning. The things I saw in my dream were **symbols**. Here is what those symbols mean and how this dream can help you.

The tree is **God's love** (1 Nephi 11:21–23).

To eat the fruit is to **feel Heavenly Father's love** for you. It's the best feeling in the world!

The mists of darkness are **temptations** (1 Nephi 12:17),

the huge building is **pride** and **worldliness** (1 Nephi 11:36),

and the filthy river is **sin** (1 Nephi 12:16),

. . . all of which keep us from feeling **God's love** (eating the fruit).

There's only one way to make it past all those bad influences—HOLD FAST to the IRON ROD!

And the IRON ROD is the **word of God** (1 Nephi 15:23–24).

The **word of God** comes from the **scriptures,** the **words of the prophets and apostles**, and **the Holy Ghost**.

We HOLD FAST to the **word of God** when we *do* what the scriptures and the prophets tell us to do and when we obey the promptings of the Holy Ghost.

How can YOU be like Lehi and his family?

When you HOLD to the ROD, you won't be tempted to make bad choices.

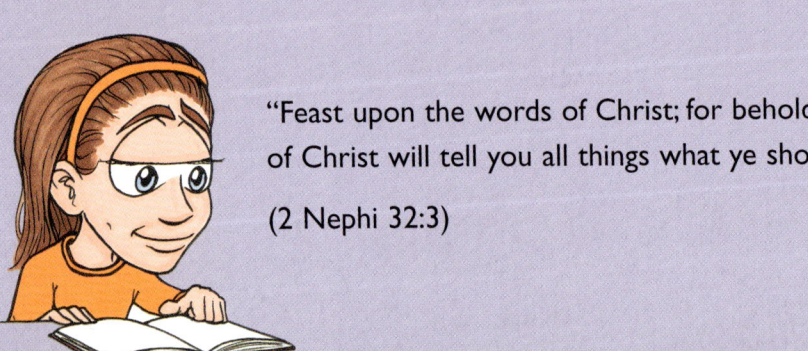

"Feast upon the words of Christ; for behold, the words of Christ will tell you all things what ye should do."

(2 Nephi 32:3)

When you HOLD to the ROD, you won't feel like you *have* to *have* all the latest and greatest toys.

"The scriptures are full of warnings against worldliness and pride because they can lead us off the course that leads to eternal life."

(Elder L. Tom Perry, "'Give Heed unto the Word of the Lord,'" *Ensign,* June 2000, 26)

When you HOLD to the ROD, you won't be ashamed or embarrassed if people make fun of you for your beliefs.

"For I am not ashamed of the gospel of Christ: for it is the power of God unto salvation to every one that believeth."

(Romans 1:16)

When you HOLD to the ROD and stay away from Satan's influences, you will feel Heavenly Father's love for you. You will be happy and know you are doing the right thing.

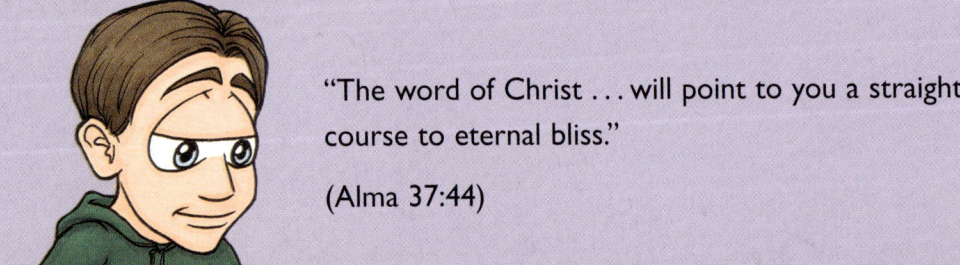

"The word of Christ . . . will point to you a straight course to eternal bliss."

(Alma 37:44)

FHE Lesson Helps for Lehi's Family Holds Fast to the Word of God

Songs and Hymns

Children's Songbook:
"Book of Mormon Stories," 118–19 (additional verse by David Bowman)

> *Lehi had a dream one night that's meant for you and me:*
> *Holding to an iron rod he made it to a tree.*
> *Its fruit he ate, it tasted great, he knew the iron rod*
> *For you and me had to be the Word of God.*

"Search, Ponder, and Pray," 109
"Follow the Prophet," 110–11

The Friend:
"Scripture Power," Clive Romney, October 1987, 10–11

LDS Hymns:
"The Iron Rod," no. 274
"As I Search the Holy Scriptures," no. 277
"Thy Holy Word," no. 279

Scriptures on Holding Fast to the Word of God

Joshua 1:8
2 Timothy 3:16
1 Nephi 15:23–24
Alma 31:5
Helaman 3:29

Other Scripture Stories on This Topic

Alma and the sons of Mosiah search the scriptures diligently on their missions (Alma 17:1–4)

Quotes from General Authorities

"I hope that for you [scripture study] . . . will become something far more enjoyable than a duty. . . . I promise you that as you read, your minds will be enlightened and your spirits will be lifted."
    President Gordon B. Hinckley
    "The Light within You," *Ensign,* May 1995, 99

"I plead with you to make time for immersing yourselves in the scriptures. Couple scripture study with your prayers."
    Elder M. Russell Ballard
    "Be Strong in the Lord and in the Power of His Might," CES Fireside for Young Adults, 3 March 2002

Stories and Messages from *The Friend* Magazine

"The Right Path," Ray Goldrup, May 2006, 36–39

"Hold On," Elizabeth Giles, September 2006, 11

Activities

Lehi Says . . .
This is a good old-fashioned game of Simon (in this case, Lehi) Says. To play this game, every family member needs to have a Book of Mormon or set of scriptures. Dad will act as "Lehi." The first thing he says is "Lehi says . . . Pick up your scriptures and don't let go." Then he makes several "Lehi says" statements (whatever Dad comes up with). After a while he tries to trick them with "set your book down at your feet" or "put your scriptures on the couch," without saying "Lehi says." Play as long as you'd like, periodically trying to get them to let go of their books.

Discussion: Lehi is a prophet, and prophets always encourage us to Hold to the Iron Rod (the scriptures) and never let go. In other words, if someone or something tries to get you to disobey the commandments (to let go of the iron rod or the word of God), then you can know that that influence is coming from Satan and you should not listen. If you will follow what "Lehi (the prophet) says," you will be safe. Use pages 12–13 of this book to help with the discussion.

Find the Fruit
Beforehand, hide one piece of fruit for each family member in or by various locations in the house listed below (pick locations that apply to your house). During the activity, give each family member a secret code of numbers indicating where their fruit is hidden. Tell them they will use the word of God in 1 Nephi 8 (Lehi's vision) to decipher the code and discover the clue words needed to find their fruit. Then teach them the key to breaking the code: 1st number = the verse in chapter 8, 2nd number = the line in that verse, 3rd number = the word in that line.

    13–4–1, 20–5–4 (kitchen sink)
    24–2–2, 19–1–7 (clothing iron)
    14–4–6, 27–3–6 (Mom's dresses/closet)
    2–2–2, 5–3–2 (Dad's bathrobe pocket)
    19–1–5, 8–5–2, 13–1–4 (fishing pole)
    2–2–2, 30–1–6 (Dad's desk)
    30–1–4, 21–2–3, 26–4–2 (doll house/action figure castle)
    2–2–2, 14–4–1, 2–4–2 (Dad's pillow)

Once everyone has found his or her fruit, eat it together in the family room. Discuss how delicious it is, how it is "like feeling God's love for us and how much we want to work together as a family to feel God's love in our home." Also discuss how it was only by following God's word (the secret code) that you were able to find His love (the fruit).

Word Search
On page 73 of this book is a WORD SEARCH of different sources where we can find the word of God. Children can work together to solve the puzzle in the book or you can make copies for them to do individually. Discuss with them how each of these sources (books, people, etc.) can reveal God's word to us today.

AMULEK and ALMA
Cooperate

One day I was traveling to visit a relative when an angel suddenly appeared! "Amulek," he said, "return to your house, for you are going to feed a prophet of God. He is hungry and needs your help." I did what the angel told me to do. (Alma 10:7–8)

On my way home, I met the prophet, just like the angel said I would. His name was Alma and he had not had anything to eat for many days. I took him to my house and invited him to have dinner with us. He was very grateful. (Alma 8:19–20)

Alma ate dinner with my family and thanked us for being so kind to him. He said that he was commanded to help the people in my city repent of their wickedness. "And God wants *you*, Amulek, to preach with me and be my companion," Alma told me. I accepted the call. (Alma 8:21–29)

Alma and I went into the city and began talking to the people. We told them of the coming of Jesus Christ and that they needed to repent and turn to Jesus. The people were very prideful and did not want to hear this. (Alma 8:32; 9:1–8, 31–34)

Since we were companions, we took turns preaching to the people. Alma and I worked together to share God's message. (Alma 9:1–6, 34; 10:12; 12:1)

But even then they would not listen to us. Instead they were angry and threw Alma and me into prison. (Alma 14:2–4, 17)

We were in prison for many days. The wicked judges and priests mocked us. They hit us on our cheeks and gave us very little food and water. Alma and I supported each other during this very difficult time. (Alma 14:18–24)

After many days of this, the Lord filled us with his power. We stood up and Alma cried out, "O Lord, give us strength, according to our faith in Christ, to break these chains!" We snapped our chains and the whole prison began to shake! The judges and priests tried to escape, but the prison walls fell on top of them. (Alma 14:25–27)

Alma and I were the only ones to walk out of the collapsed prison. The Lord had kept us safe.

(Alma 14:28–29)

After that, Alma returned the kindness I had shown to him. He took me to *his* house and fed *me*. We had suffered so much together. It was nice to have a friend who cared. (Alma 15:16, 18)

Alma and I spent several years together as missionary companions. It was our job to go all over the land teaching the gospel of Jesus Christ. We were able to help many people because we knew how to COOPERATE with each other and work together. (Alma 16:13–15)

How can YOU be like Amulek and Alma?

Show kindness to everyone, even to people you don't know well. They will usually be kind to you in return.

Learn how to take turns with people . . . and be happy when it's their turn also.

Help other people even when things are stressful. Those are the times when we especially need to COOPERATE and not argue.

Any job can be fun when you work together and COOPERATE. And it sure makes the job easier!

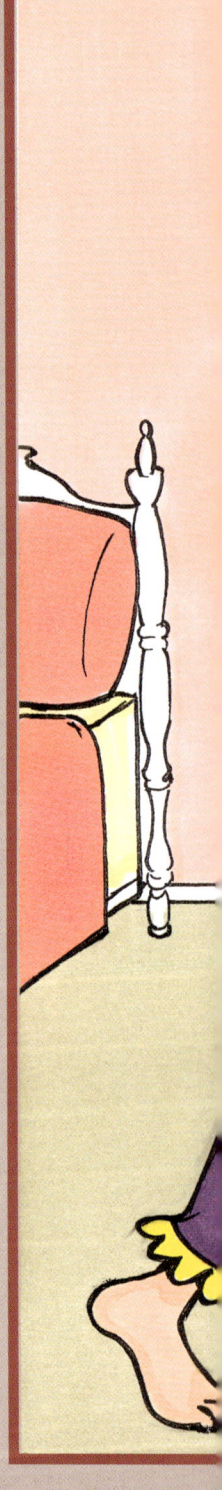

FHE Lesson Helps for Amulek and Alma Cooperate

Songs and Hymns

Children's Songbook:
"Book of Mormon Stories," 118–19 (additional verse by David Bowman)

> Amulek and Alma were great mission companions.
> Preaching side by side, they worked until the job was done.
> Cooperation was the key to their great success.
> They showed us that team work works the BEST!

"A Happy Helper," 197
"I'll Walk with You," 140–41
"Kindness Begins with Me," 145

LDS Hymns:
"Let Us Oft Speak Kind Words," no. 232
"As Sisters in Zion," no. 309
"Love at Home," no. 294

Scriptures on Cooperating

Proverbs 18:24
1 Peter 3:8
Mosiah 2:17
3 Nephi 11:29
Moses 7:18

Other Scripture Stories on This Topic

David's and Jonathan's friendship (1 Samuel 18:1–4; 19:1–5; 20:4, 17)

The people of Nephi live in a spirit of cooperation (2 Nephi 5:9–18, 26–27)

Quotes from General Authorities

"Kindness is a passport that opens doors and fashions friends. It softens hearts and molds relationships that can last lifetimes."
  Elder Joseph B. Wirthlin
  "The Virtue of Kindness," *Ensign,* May 2005, 26

"Be that kind of friend and that kind of person who lifts and strengthens others."
  Elder Robert D. Hales
  "Gifts of the Spirit," *Ensign,* February 2002, 12

Stories and Messages from *The Friend* Magazine

"Getting Pushy on the Pond," Jean Leedale Hobson, January 2008, 46–47

"Who Is My Neighbor?" Ruth Kathryn Day, August 2007, 42–43

Activities

Let's Cooperate
Adjust these fun, simple cooperation activities for the size of your family. When you are finished doing them, discuss how working together to succeed at the games is much like the need for working together to succeed as a family.

Human Pyramid: You know how to do this one. Be careful who goes on which layer of the pyramid!

Three-or-More-Legged Race: A three-legged race is fun, but how much more fun (and more cooperation is needed) to succeed in a four-, five-, six-, or more-legged race!

Wheelbarrow Race: You know how to do this one, too. Be careful that the person pushing the wheelbarrow-person doesn't push too hard or too fast.

Feed Your Neighbor: Seated in a circle, eat dinner or dessert with each person's plate placed halfway between him or her and the person to their left. For the entire meal, each person has to feed the person to his left. No one is allowed to feed himself!

String Carry: Using only a piece of string, one person tries picking up an object (a block, book, etc.) by balancing the object on top of the stretched-out string. When he fails, try picking up the object the same way using two people and two pieces of string. Then try it with three, four, or five people—as many family members as you have (each adding another string). Each added person and string should make the task easier, giving more support underneath the object. Try carrying the object across the room.

Got Your Back: Sitting or standing in a circle, everyone gives the person in front of them a shoulder rub or back scratch. Aaahh, that feels good!

Back Stand: Have family members sit on the floor in pairs, back to back, and try to stand up using no arms but only the pressure from the other person's back. After successfully doing it in pairs, try it in groups of three, four, five, etc.

Puzzling Family
On a single sheet of paper, each family member draws a quick picture of himself or herself. Once the family portrait masterpiece is completed, Mom or Dad cuts the picture into pieces, writes one of the Scriptures on Cooperating* on the back of each piece, and gives one piece to each person. Family members look up their scriptures, taking turns reading them out loud and explaining what they mean to them. Then, one by one, they put their pieces back down, eventually completing the puzzle and putting the family back together! List specific ways your family could cooperate better. After family home evening, tape the picture pieces together and hang the portrait on the fridge as a reminder that "we don't want to be a separate-pieces family, but a joined-together family!"

* Other good scriptures are Colossians 3:19, 21 (for Dad's piece of the puzzle), Mosiah 4:14–15 (for Mom's piece), and Colossians 3:20 (for one of the children).

MORMON and MORONI
Act Responsibly

Hello, my friend. My name is Mormon. And this is my son, Moroni. We were given some very important assignments from the Lord. God needed us to ACT RESPONSIBLY in these assignments so that one day you would have a record of our people. Here's our story.

When I was ten years old, the prophet Ammaron saw that I was a responsible child who could be trusted. He told me of a hill that had all the sacred records of our people stored inside. "When you are 24 years old," he said, "go find this hill and take out the plates of Nephi. The Lord needs you to write a record of this people on those plates." I promised him I would do it. (Mormon 1:2–5)

I lived in a time of great wickedness. Neither the Lamanites nor the Nephites were keeping God's commandments. When I was only sixteen, the people chose me to be the leader of their armies. I loved my people and wanted to serve them, even though they had forgotten the Lord. (Mormon 2:1–2)

For many years I remembered the promise I had made to Ammaron. When I was old enough, I found the hill he had told me about. I took the plates of Nephi and began writing a history of our people.

(Mormon 2:17)

I spent the rest of my life leading the Nephite armies. I was sad because I knew the Lord was not with us anymore. I encouraged my people to repent, but they would not listen. All they wanted to do was fight the Lamanites. (Mormon 3:1–3, 12)

During those years of war, I wrote the history of our people on the gold plates. I wrote about all the great Nephite heroes of the past. I wrote about our Savior, Jesus Christ, and how we need to follow Him. I did the best job I could and made a very thorough record. This needed to be a special book for anyone who read it. (Mormon 3:20–22)

One terrible day, the largest Lamanite army I had ever seen gathered to attack us. I was old by this time and I knew this would be our last battle. I gave the gold plates to my son, Moroni, to take care of and to keep safe from the Lamanites. (Mormon 6:6–8)

I, Moroni, will finish the story. All the Nephites except me were killed in that terrible battle, including my father, Mormon. I was now alone. I was very sad, but I knew I had to finish the job my father had given me and protect the gold plates. (Mormon 8:1–3)

For many, many years, I wandered across the land. I was very lonely. But I continued to keep the gold plates safe from the Lamanites, even though there was no one reminding me to do it. (Mormon 8:5–8)

I knew when it was time to bury the plates. But before I did, I wrote a promise to future generations. I promised them that if they would read this book, think about how much Jesus loves them, and ask Heavenly Father if the book is true, the Holy Ghost would let them know that it is true. (Moroni 10:1–5)

I took the gold plates to a hill called Cumorah and buried them in the ground. For all our lives, my father and I wrote on the plates and took care of them. Now I trusted that Heavenly Father would keep them safe in the earth until someone in the future would be led to find them. (Mormon 8:4; Title Page of the Book of Mormon)

And that person was a young man named Joseph Smith. Over 1,000 years later, I appeared as an angel to Joseph and showed him where the gold plates were. Through God's power, he was able to translate them into the Book of Mormon, Another Testament of Jesus Christ. Because my father and I ACTED RESPONSIBLY, you are able to enjoy the Book of Mormon today. (Introduction to the Book of Mormon)

How can YOU be like Mormon and Moroni?

Remember to do the jobs you are given.

Responsible people can be counted on!

Always do your very best work, whether cleaning your room, doing your homework, or any other task. Responsible people do a thorough job.

Do what you are supposed to without having to be reminded. Responsible people are self-motivated.

As Latter-day Saints, we have a responsibility with the Book of Mormon. Heavenly Father wants us to read it, pray about it, share it with others, and live by what it teaches. You can do all of these things!

FHE Lesson Helps for Mormon and Moroni Act Responsibly

Songs and Hymns

Children's Songbook:
"Book of Mormon Stories," 118–19 (additional verse by David Bowman)

> *Mormon wrote on golden plates a very sacred book.*
> *Then his son Moroni to a hill the plates he took*
> *'Cause they were responsible we have that book today.*
> *The Book of Mormon shows us the way.*

"Go the Second Mile," 167
"An Angel Came to Joseph Smith," 86
"The Golden Plates," 86

LDS Hymns:
"An Angel from on High," no. 13
"I Have Work Enough to Do," no. 224
"Put Your Shoulder to the Wheel," no. 252

Scriptures on Acting Responsibly

Proverbs 22:29
Colossians 3:23
Alma 53:20
D&C 58:26–27
D&C 75:3

Other Scripture Stories on This Topic

Nephi sticking to the task of obtaining the brass plates from Laban (1 Nephi 3–4)

Joseph Smith taking good care of the golden plates (JS–H 1:59–60)

Quotes from General Authorities

"Honesty and integrity are not old-fashioned principles. . . . In our dealings with both God and our fellowmen, let us be examples of honesty and integrity."
Elder Sheldon F. Child
"As Good As Our Bond," *Ensign,* May 1997, 29–30

"We cannot be less than honest, we cannot be less than true . . . if we are to keep sacred the trust given us."
President Gordon B. Hinckley
"We Believe in Being Honest," *Ensign,* October 1990, 5

Stories and Messages from *The Friend* Magazine

"Popularity or Responsibility?" Lauren N., June 2007, 28

"Ben Obeys," Elizabeth Hervey Osborn, October 2006, 30–32

Activities

Stick to It!
President Thomas S. Monson has a favorite quote that teaches us to act responsibly:

> *Stick to your task 'til it sticks to you;*
> *Beginners are many, but enders are few.*
> *Honor, power, place and praise*
> *Will come, in time, to the one who stays.*
> *Stick to your task 'til it sticks to you;*
> *Bend at it, sweat at it, smile at it, too;*
> *For out of the bend and the sweat and the smile*
> *Will come life's victories, after awhile.*

(*Favorite Quotations from the Collection of Thomas S. Monson* [Salt Lake City: Deseret Book Co., 1985], 157)

Discuss the quote and memorize it as a family (shortening the quote as needed for younger children). Make a sign of the quote or use the sign found on page 72 to put on your refrigerator as a reminder.

Here's a fun, simple activity you can do that goes along with "sticking" to something: Each family member puts a small masking tape roll on the end of his or her nose. Then go around touching your nose to someone else's nose, trying to take the tape from the other person. See who can "stick to it" the strongest. If your tape is taken, you're out. Keep going until one person is left with all the tape rolls on his or her nose. Congratulate him or her as the "stick-to-it"-est person in the family!

I Did Keep a Record
Dad dresses up as a Book of Mormon prophet (bathrobe, a tie around the head, whatever else you can think of). Tell the children that you "perceive" they are responsible children (see Mormon 1:2), and that therefore they need to find some very special plates buried or hidden in the backyard—the paper plates. Have them find the paper plates (yes, actual kitchen paper plates) and then inform them that they need to keep a record on these plates of their responsibilities for that week (or any allotted time you choose). Children should write down their jobs on their paper plate(s) and decorate them with designs, markings, etc., to make them look authentic. During the next week(s), they personally keep track of how they did on their responsibilities and then, during a subsequent family home evening, report back to the "Nephite prophet" (Dad), who gives them some reward.

We're Responsible!
This is a fun memory game you can play with the family. Everyone sits in a circle and beats a slow pat-and-clap rhythm (pat your knees, then clap your hands). Keeping in the rhythm, everyone says "Responsible _____ [your family's last name] . . . ," then the first person says one job that someone in the family does, while making hand motions miming that job, and then everyone finishes by saying "with a BIG OL' SMILE!" flashing a cheesy grin with their fingers in the corners of their mouths. The family repeats the chant and the next person in the circle adds another job (with hand motions) and everyone finishes "with a BIG OL' SMILE!" Only the person adding a job does the hand motions; everyone else pats and claps the rhythm. Keep going around the circle, adding one job at a time, until it's just too hard to remember THAT many jobs! Remember to keep everything in time with the pat-and-clap rhythm. Here's an example:

"Responsible Bowmans . . . clean their room . . . with a BIG OL' SMILE!"
   (pat)   (clap)   (pat) (clap)   (cheesy grin)
"Responsible Bowmans . . . clean their room . . . feed the dog . . . with a BIG OL' SMILE!"
   (pat)   (clap)   (pat) (clap)   (pat) (clap)   (cheesy grin)

Stick to It!

Stick to your task 'til it sticks to you;

Beginners are many, but enders are few.

Honor, power, place and praise

Will come, in time, to the one who stays.

Stick to your task 'til it sticks to you;

Bend at it, sweat at it, smile at it, too;

For out of the bend and the sweat and the smile

Will come life's victories, after awhile.

Favorite Quotations from the Collection of Thomas S. Monson
[Salt Lake City: Deseret Book Co., 1985], 157

Word Search

S	O	C	J	I	H	A	M	O	B	I	E	T	S	A
R	T	A	P	O	W	D	A	N	D	C	L	P	E	P
U	M	I	G	O	F	B	Z	P	N	Q	O	R	L	Y
A	W	F	C	R	H	I	I	E	U	M	C	B	T	U
P	P	U	R	O	L	B	R	S	E	P	D	I	S	K
N	E	L	T	I	N	E	M	E	H	R	E	B	O	N
O	A	A	V	P	F	O	N	Z	S	O	O	L	P	B
F	R	I	E	N	D	C	R	D	I	P	P	G	A	L
R	L	D	O	T	M	Y	E	E	C	H	M	O	S	E
I	A	C	B	D	O	L	O	O	V	E	O	T	Z	S
E	D	B	H	I	B	X	A	A	P	T	T	Y	I	S
N	R	O	M	I	R	A	U	L	E	B	P	A	D	I
N	E	F	B	O	O	K	O	F	M	O	R	M	O	N
O	N	O	I	T	A	L	E	V	E	R	L	J	O	G
T	D	A	I	B	S	H	O	N	O	P	E	C	A	S

Different sources where we can find the word of God:

PROPHET
APOSTLES
(General) CONFERENCE
BIBLE
BOOK OF MORMON
D AND C
PEARL (of Great Price)
FRIEND (magazine)
REVELATION
MEN
BISHOP

Also get
Who's Your Hero?
Volumes 1, 2, and 3

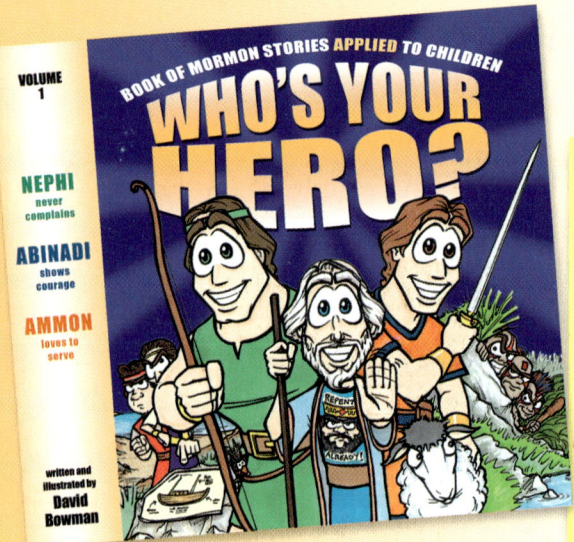

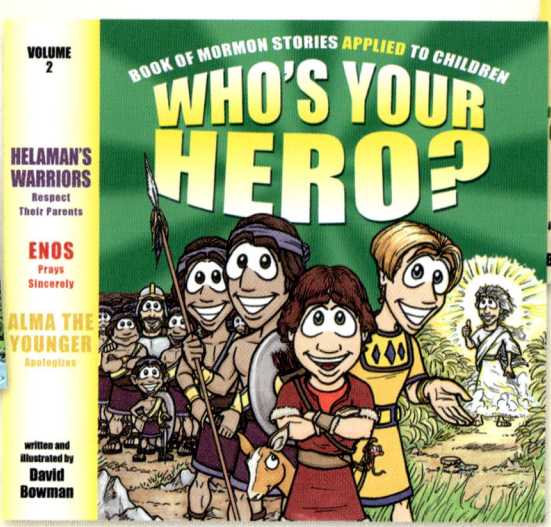

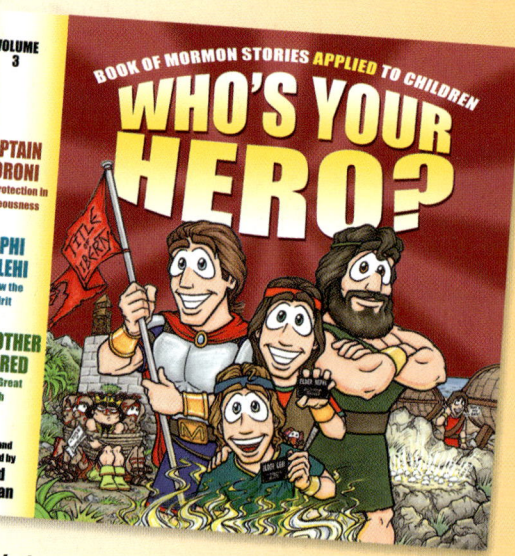

Volume 1
Teaches about not complaining, showing courage, and loving to serve

Volume 2
Teaches about respecting parents, praying sincerely, and apologizing

Volume 3
Teaches about finding protection in righteousness, following the Spirit, and showing faith

To see more of David Bowman's Book of Mormon caricatures go to www.bowman-art.com.